GW00645519

Preparing for Your Child's Baptism

by
Sr Hyacinthe Defos du Rau, OP

All booklets are published thanks to the generous support of the members of the Catholic Truth Society

CATHOLIC TRUTH SOCIETY
PUBLISHERS TO THE HOLY SEE

Contents

All rights reserved. First published 2014 by The Incorporated Catholic Truth Society, 40-46 Harleyford Road London SE11 5AY Tel: 020 7640 0042 Fax: 020 7640 0046. Rite of Baptism © ICEL. © 2014 The Incorporated Catholic Truth Society.

ISBN 978 1 78469 006 9

Introduction

Dear parents,

You have been given a wonderful gift, entrusted to you: your child. Now you are considering baptism for your child, or have already asked for your child to be baptised. This booklet is for you, to help you understand what you are asking for your child, and what personal commitment you will take on as a family in having your child baptised. As you read, you will discover:

- What baptism is.

- How it is celebrated.

- How it is lived day-to-day.

- How to prepare for it.

You will see that baptism is much more than a social or religious formality. It is a wonderful gift of New Life given to us by God through the Church to enable us to live our life to the full, here and for all eternity. You have given birth to a new human person, your child. In asking for the new birth of baptism, you are asking God to make your child his own.

What is Baptism?

Baptism is a Gift

A gift from God

*"I have come so that they may have life
and have it to the full."* (*John* 10:10)[1]

Since you are considering or asking baptism for your child, one of you at least has received baptism and is a member of the Catholic Church. Before going ahead with baptism for your child, it is good to recall the meaning of baptism in your own life. Often we do not remember the day or even the date of our baptism. Yet on that day we received a gift from God, a gift which has enabled us to come to this day with faith and love for God and a desire to make our children sharers in God's own life of love in the Church.

Our daily life can be filled with joy and moments of great happiness, with the security and strength found in the love of our family and friends, with the delights of new and exciting experiences, in the great and small things that come our way. Yet all of us also experience the cruel reality of suffering and death, of divisions, anger, loneliness and sin. We can even be tempted to question how a loving

[1] All Scripture references are taken from *The CTS New Catholic Bible*.

God can allow such misery to take place in the world and in our own lives. Yet the evil and sin we experience is often of human origin: a refusal of love and forgiveness coupled with the rejection of others and of God in the self-glorification and self-achievement we call pride.

Baptism is a gift from God to us. It is the gift of his forgiveness of all sins: of all the sins we have ever committed, and of the mysterious mark of original sin which has wounded each one of us. Original sin in the human heart accounts for the fact that we are more easily inclined to sin than to holiness, to selfish passions than to joyful self-giving. It stifles from the start our ability to love, like seeds of fear and selfishness, hidden in our hearts, which seem to have always been there. It affects all of us.

Our Christian faith, founded on the Word of God who has come to us and has spoken to us through the ages, is built on the sure knowledge that God is love: He is Father, Son and Holy Spirit, an eternal, personal relationship of love, which we call communion. God has made us for himself, to live eternally in his presence, free from sin, death and suffering. If we examine the depth of our hearts, we can recognise this longing for a love that never ends, for peace, for joy, for life: for God himself who is love, peace, joy and life.

Baptism is the gift of God's love. Provided we have faith in him, baptism is our entry into the *communion* of Father, Son and Holy Spirit, into God's own life of love.

God's gift of himself

"I lay down my life for my sheep." (*John* 10:15)

Who is Jesus? Jesus Christ is God the Son, sent by the Father to save us. He has come into the world as man to take on himself everything that we are, and all the sin we inflict on ourselves, and to give us everything that he is. Only God can save us, and Jesus is fully God. He has taken on our human nature to make it whole again, to make it holy. We call Jesus our Saviour: he saves us from sin and death through his death on the cross and his resurrection from the dead. In his Passion and death on the cross, Jesus has taken our own sins and their consequence on himself. By rising from the dead to live eternally, he has defeated the power of sin and death over the human nature that he has taken on.

In receiving baptism with faith, we receive the salvation that Jesus, God the Son, has won for us on the cross, and we receive the new life of the resurrection that he desires to give us. Jesus has given his life for us on the cross and at the moment of baptism, we receive the gift of his life. We are changed. In Jesus, we become dead to sin and alive with a life that will endure forever with God, beyond physical death. Our part now is to remain united with him until we die.

Since in baptism we are made one with Jesus, who is God the Son, we are also made one with the Father and the Holy Spirit: we enter into God's eternal communion of love.

This is a free gift. It is a gift especially available to sinners, to those who know that they are in need of salvation: to all of us. It only requires of us a trusting heart and the humility to accept that we are in need of salvation, in need of a new life, of a fresh beginning for a life that will never end, in the love and joy of God, who is Father, Son and Holy Spirit.

Your gift to your child

A man came up to him and went down on his knees before him. "Lord," he said, "take pity on my son."
(*Matthew* 17:14-15)

Baptism is a gift which we are free to accept. God never imposes himself on anyone but respects our choices and decisions. He invites us, and has been inviting us to turn to him throughout the centuries, by sending his Son and his Holy Spirit. In asking baptism for your child, you are responding to God's invitation for your child, allowing your child to enter already the life of God, the life of grace, which will enable him or her to grow and flourish as a child of God. You are asking God to give salvation and eternal life to your child. Without you, your child wouldn't have access to this gift, because only you have the authority as parents to decide what is best for your child.

Baptism is a Call

A call to be faithful to the baptismal promises
"Follow me" (Mark 1:17)

Baptism is a gift from God, but it is also a call to live in faithfulness to God and to the Church. On the day of your child's baptism, you will be asked to make a series of personal promises. The baptismal promises, which you will make on behalf of your child, and as a commitment to bring up your child in the Catholic faith, include a renunciation of sin and a profession of faith in God who is Father, Son and Holy Spirit.[2] They are made solemnly and truthfully. Baptism is the beginning of the life of faith in the Church. By making those promises, you commit yourself to lead your child into a life of faithfulness to God and to the Church.

You can only make these promises if you believe and intend to keep them, otherwise baptism becomes meaningless. If only one of you believes and has the intention to keep these promises, this is sufficient. Anyone who cannot answer the questions of the baptismal promises with honesty must remain silent. The godparents too will be asked to make these promises in faith and sincerity. This is why it is important to choose carefully who your child's godparents will be. Will they be able to make these promises in sincerity?

---

[2] You can find the text of the baptismal promises on pp. 28-30.

The role of the godparents is very important. They are called to help you to fulfil the promises made on behalf of your child. Their role is to ensure that the promises made are kept faithfully, encouraging your child to grow and flourish not only in every human way but in the life of faith, in faithfulness to that unique relationship of God with your child, which begins at baptism.

A call to live in God

"Make your home in me, as I make mine in you."
(*John* 15:4)

The Father invites us to enter into a friendship with him, an encounter of love which he makes possible through the sending of his Son Jesus Christ and of the Holy Spirit into our hearts. All is provided for this encounter to take place, but it cannot happen without us. Our decision to respond to God's invitation of love begins with baptism and needs to be carried out through our life, until we die: this is the full meaning of the baptismal promises. Once we are baptised, we renew our baptismal promises year after year at Easter as a sign of our commitment to God's enduring faithfulness towards us.

How can we be faithful to our baptismal promises? Simply by being faithful to God. This means first that we are called to be faithful to our relationship with God which begins at baptism. As parents, this will mean that we are called to foster this relationship with God in the life of our child. This will be impossible to do if we do not have a relationship with God ourselves. We can only pass on what we ourselves have received. The faith of the child will be nourished by the parents' own faith.

So in order for the child to have a relationship with God, the parents (or the parent who believes in God) need to foster their own relationship with God. This is done through regular prayer - time spent with God alone and as a family - attending church, nourishing our Catholic faith, and living a life of self-giving love. Like any relationship, our relationship with God needs time and effort to flourish.

A call to live in the Church

"I pray not only for these, but for those also who through their words will believe in me.May they all be one.
Father, may they be one in us, as you are in me and I am in you, so that the world may believe that you have sent me." (John 17:20-21)

Life in communion with Father, Son and Holy Spirit - which begins at baptism - is offered to us in the Church: we cannot be in communion with God unless we are in communion with each other, in the same relationship of a love which is all inclusive. As the child entered a natural family at birth, so at baptism the child enters into the supernatural family of the Church: God's own family.

Receiving baptism means that we enter this new family in which we are nourished with God's own life and love through the sacraments and through our fellowship with each other. Once we enter a family, we are meant to live in it and not spend the rest of our life in isolation. In the same way, desiring baptism means that we desire to share in the fullness of the life of the Church, not just pass the threshold and return from where we have come.

By asking baptism, we commit to living the life of the Church, actively belonging to the community of believers. This means attending Mass on Sunday and receiving the sacraments: confirmation, confession, Holy Communion, marriage, sacrament of the sick. This means forming bonds of fellowship and friendship with other members of the Church and getting involved in activities which will help us to keep our baptismal promises. As parents, this means introducing our child into the Church, so that the Church becomes an essential part of the life of the family.

A call to holiness

"Be perfect just as your heavenly Father is perfect."
(Matthew 5:48)

What happens when we have received baptism but have failed to be faithful to God? Can we turn back to him?

God is always calling us to him. He always wants us. He never gives up on us, even if we can be tempted to give up on ourselves. His mercy is infinite, and is constantly available for us to receive in the Church through the sacrament of reconciliation or confession. This is what Pope Francis tells us about baptism and confession:

"In the Sacrament of Baptism all sins are remitted, original sin and all of our personal sins, as well as the suffering of sin. With Baptism the door to an effectively new life is opened, one which is not burdened by the weight of a negative past, but rather already feels the beauty and the goodness of the Kingdom of Heaven. It is the powerful intervention of God's mercy in our lives, to save us. This saving intervention does not take away our human nature and its weakness - we are all weak and we are all sinners - and it does not take from us our responsibility to ask for forgiveness every time we err! I cannot be baptised many times, but I can go to Confession and by doing so renew the grace of Baptism. It is as though I were being baptised for a second time. The Lord Jesus is very very good and never tires of forgiving us. Even when the door that Baptism opens to us in order to enter the Church is a little closed, due to our weaknesses and our sins. Confession reopens it, precisely because it is a second Baptism that forgives us of everything and illuminates us to go forward with the light of the Lord. Let us go forward in this way, joyfully, because life should be lived with the joy of Jesus Christ; and this is a grace of the Lord". (Pope Francis, General Audience, 13th November 2013)

We should never be afraid to find a priest who is there for us as a minister of God's mercy and forgiveness. The priest will help any baptised Catholic to make an honest confession of sins without fear, no matter how long it has been since the last one. As parents, an essential part of our task will be to help our children understand and trust the infinite mercy of God. This infinite mercy is something we are invited to experience for ourselves time and again in the sacrament of reconciliation with God. This is the source of hope in our life. God constantly offers us a fresh beginning.

Baptism Gives Us a New Identity

Child of the Father

Before the world was made, he chose us, chose us in Christ...determining that we should become his adopted sons, through Jesus Christ. (Ephesians 1:4-5)

Baptism gives us a new identity: it makes a change in us. We come to baptism as God's beloved creatures, and we come out as his beloved children. Through faith and baptism, God offers us salvation from sin, and he offers us an even greater gift: a new identity, a new being, a new form of life, which is eternal. God desires to makes each one of us his child. We are free to respond to this invitation. It is in baptism that we become children of the Father.

Parents 'beget' ('generate' or 'produce') children of the same kind, of the same nature: a pair of cats begets another cat, a pair of birds begets another bird, a man and a woman beget a human person. At baptism, we are mysteriously 'begotten' by God: God the Father adopts us as his children and makes us "share the divine nature" (*2 Peter* 1:4), the very nature of God himself. We receive the life and the love of God in such a way that we are made able to respond to God's love with love, and share in the communion of love of Father, Son and Holy Spirit. We enter into a relationship of friendship and reciprocity, because God's grace makes us capable of knowing and loving him as our Father.

The prayer of the *Our Father*, which is given to us by Jesus, is the prayer of all the baptised, of all those who have been adopted as children of the Father through faith and baptism. As children of God, we can relate to him more closely and intimately than we could ever have imagined. Through the Holy Spirit, we can now call God 'Abba', which means 'Daddy'.

One with the Son

But you, God has made members of Christ Jesus and by God's doing he has become our wisdom, and our virtue, and our holiness, and our freedom. (1 *Corinthians* 1:30)

We become children of the Father at baptism because baptism makes us one with Jesus, who is the only begotten Son of the Father. If we are one with the Son, then we are children of the Father: 'sons in the Son'. God the Son, Jesus Christ, has come to share our humanity so that we may share in his divinity, in his divine nature. United with him we enter the communion of Father, Son and Holy Spirit: the life of the Holy Trinity, now and forever.

This union with Jesus Christ is made possible by his sacrifice for us on the cross and his resurrection from the dead. Through the cross and resurrection, he takes away the sin that separates us from him and offers us a share in his risen life. The cross stands as the greatest sign of the love of God who chooses to die and give his life in sacrifice rather than have us be separated from him because of our sins. He takes on our sins, our death, and gives us his life. We receive this life of Jesus in the Church.

This union with Jesus Christ, which happens at baptism and grows throughout our life until it is fully actualised in heaven, is nourished every time we receive the Body and Blood of Christ at Mass. He has become one with us and we choose to become one with him by receiving him more and more into ourselves, and responding to his love with our love, through prayer and self-giving to others.

Temple of the Holy Spirit

Your body, you know, is the temple of the Holy Spirit,
who is in you since you received him from God.
(*1 Corinthians* 6:19)

At baptism we are made one with Jesus because we are filled with God the Holy Spirit who unites us with him. The Holy Spirit is 'God within us'. The Father and the Son have sent the Holy Spirit into the Church at Pentecost, and he has remained with us ever since. He comes and fills the hearts of those who call upon him and are open to his joyful presence.

The Holy Spirit is the third Person of God the Blessed Trinity. He proceeds from the Father and the Son. He is the Love of the Father and the Son. He is the 'Gift' of God and the 'Giver of Life'.

Through his cross and resurrection, the Son has reconciled us with the Father by uniting us with him. The bond of unity we have with Jesus Christ is the Holy Spirit - the Person of the Love of God. The Holy Spirit is sent on us on the day of our baptism and fills us with the love of the Father and the Son. He unites us to God and to each other. It is the Holy Spirit dwelling in our hearts who enables us to live as Jesus lived, to love as Jesus loved, and to obey the commandments of love that Jesus has given us. It is through the Holy Spirit that we remain in Jesus. We can call on the Holy Spirit every day, to come and fill our hearts and conform us more and more to the likeness of Jesus, as children of the Father. It is only through the power of the Holy Spirit dwelling in us that we are able to fulfil the call of our baptism. God never asks us to do something that is beyond our power. He gives us his own power - the Holy Spirit - to enable us to live our Christian life. As parents, it will be our responsibility to introduce familiarity with the Holy Spirit in the home and in the life of our children.

Member of the Church

Now you together as Christ's body; but each of you is a different part of it (1 *Corinthians* 12:27)

Baptism unites us with God and therefore it unites us with one another. This unity, or communion of the children of the Father in Jesus and through the Holy Spirit is called the Church. Through baptism we become members of the Church, members of the Body of Christ, forever. We enter a fellowship of faith and charity which has no boundaries in space or in time, except the boundary of sin, which is harmful to this unity and can even be a self-exclusion from this fellowship, from this communion.

The Church has no boundaries in space. The Church is Catholic, which means 'universal'. It is open to everyone, everywhere, with no restriction of language or culture.

The Church has no boundaries in time. It includes all people - all the baptised who are in communion with God and with each other, both living and dead. The saints in heaven and those who have gone before us 'marked with the sign of faith' all are joined to the Body of the risen Christ. They are alive in him, and belong to the living Church. Through baptism we are part of this 'communion of the saints' and we can ask and rely on the prayers of the saints who see God face-to-face.

As baptised members of the Church, united in faith and love and in the visible bonds of communion with the Pope and bishops who are the successors of the Apostles, the other sacraments of the Church are available to us, to help us grow in unity with God and with each other throughout our lives.

How is Baptism Celebrated?[3]

This section will help you to understand what will happen during your child's baptism. You will find a summary and explanation of the main parts of baptism, which can be celebrated during Mass or outside of Mass. The ceremony of baptism, whether it is celebrated within Mass or outside of Mass, always begins with the sign of the cross. The sign of the cross is the sign of the baptised, of those who belong to Christ and know that the cross is now the doorway to life and the sign of God's love. The sign of the cross is made in the name of the Father and of the Son and of the Holy Spirit.

The name

"I have called you by name, you are mine." (Isaiah 43:1)

Before all else, the parents who come forward for the baptism of their child are asked:

What name have you given your child?

Our Christian name is of infinite value. It is spoken at our baptism. My name signifies who I am. A Christian name

---

[3] All the quotations from the rite of baptism are taken from the English translation of the *Rite of Baptism for Children* ©1969, International Commission on English in the Liturgy Corporation. All rights reserved. Confirmed by the Congregation for Divine Worship, 15th April 1970, Prot. No. 1667/70.

points to an unrepeatable person, uniquely willed and created by God through the co-operation - the 'pro-creation' - of the parents. God knows my name and calls me by name, he knows each one of us personally. God has revealed his own name to us in Jesus Christ: he is Father, Son and Holy Spirit. We too can call God by name, in an exchange of love and friendship with him. In the same way, parents entrust their child to God by name. Uniquely and lovingly created, the child is called by name to enter into the family of God and be born to eternal life through baptism.

The parents' solemn request and responsibility
"Still happier those who hear the word of God and keep it!" (*Luke* 11:28)

Then the priest asks the parents:

What do you ask of God's Church for **N.**? The parents answer: **Baptism**.

No child can be baptised without the parents' consent. The Church does not impose her faith and practice on anyone. Parents come freely ask that their child be received in the Church, and so freely take on the responsibility of ensuring that their child will be an active member of the Church. The parents and godparents therefore make a free and public commitment to bring up their child in the faith. This serious commitment can only be made sincerely. Here is what the parents promise to do:

You have asked to have your child baptised. In doing so you are accepting the responsibility of training him/her in the practice of the faith. It will be your duty to bring him/her up to keep God's commandments as Christ taught us, by loving God and our neighbour. Do you clearly understand what you are undertaking?

The parents answer: **We do.**

The priest will then ask the godparents:

Are you ready to help the parents of this child in their duty as Christian parents? The godparents answer: **We are**.

Reflecting on these words will help parents and godparents to come to a deeper understanding of what they are asking for their child and what they are committing themselves to. This responsibility of bringing up their child in the faith includes the commitment of attending Mass every Sunday, of praying together as a family and teaching the child to pray, and of educating the child to act and live in love of God and neighbour.

The tracing of the cross

"If anyone wants to be a follower of mine, let him renounce himself and take up his cross and follow me."
(*Matthew* 16:24)

Once the parents have made their request and publicly affirmed their intention of bringing up their child in the faith, the priest welcomes the child into the Christian community and marks the child with the sign of the cross:

N., *the Christian community welcomes you with great joy.*

In its name I claim you for Christ our Saviour by the sign of his cross.

I now trace the cross on your forehead and invite your parents and godparents to do the same.

The name Christian comes from 'Christ'. It is the name of those who belong to Christ, who have come to believe in Christ, have been claimed by Christ and are redeemed by his blood poured out for us on the cross. The cross is the sign of salvation. This is why Christians often wear a cross or a crucifix as a sign of their love and faith in Christ, and why a cross or a crucifix are often seen hanging on the wall of a Christian home. A crucifix is a cross on which the body of Jesus (the *corpus*) is carved and displayed. A good present for the newly baptised could be a beautiful cross or crucifix to be hung in his or her room.

By tracing the cross on the child's forehead, the priest claims the child for Jesus Christ. The parents and godparents also trace this sign, as it shows their faith in Jesus Christ and their intention and commitment to place their child under the protection of the cross of Christ.

The celebration of God's Word

At various times in the past and in various different ways,
God spoke to our ancestors through the prophets;
but in our own time...he has spoken to us through his Son.
(Hebrews 1:1-2)

Passages from Holy Scripture are read at this point. God speaks to us in his Word. One of the readings will be taken from the Gospels, which are the accounts of the life of Jesus. If the readings are especially chosen for the baptism ceremony, they will shed light on the meaning of baptism. Holy Scripture has been written under the inspiration of the Holy Spirit. Holy Scripture is the Word of God, given to us for us to know him, place our trust in him and come to love him as he loves us. It is by reading the Scripture that we discover the person of Jesus Christ and the depth of his love for us.

The priest will then give a homily: he will preach on the readings and on the meaning of baptism, explaining the Word of God and encouraging us to put it in practice in our lives.

After the homily, everyone is invited to offer prayers of intercession - bidding prayers - asking for God's blessing on the child who is to be baptised.

The invocation of the saints

May he enlighten the eyes of your mind so that you can see what hope his call holds for you, what rich glories he has promised the saints will inherit (Ephesians 1:18)

It is a custom of the Church to ask the prayers of the saints for the person who is to be baptised. This is done by praying a 'litany': calling on a number of saints who are significant in the Church: our Blessed Mother Mary, St John the Baptist, St Joseph, St Peter and St Paul...but also of saints who are significant to the person being baptised and to the family: the patron saint of the child who is to be baptised, saints after whom the family members and godparents are named, or for whom they may have a special devotion or love. By asking the saints to pray for us, we entrust ourselves and the child to their care. We ask the communion of saints - our family in heaven - to be with our child, to protect and strengthen our child as a baptised member of Jesus Christ by their prayers.

The prayer of exorcism

He cured many people of diseases and afflictions and of evil spirits, and gave the gift of sight to many who were blind. (Luke 7:21)

The prayer of exorcism prepares the child for the coming of new life in baptism, asking God to remove any trace of sin and to come and dwell within the child:

Almighty and ever-living God, you sent your only Son into the world to cast out the power of Satan, spirit of evil, to deliver us from the kingdom of darkness, and bring us into the splendour of your kingdom of light. We pray for this child: set him/her free from original sin, make him/her a temple of your glory, and send your Holy Spirit to dwell within him/her. Through Christ our Lord. **Amen.**

'Exorcism' means the casting out of evil powers. Praying this important prayer before baptism does not imply that the person is possessed or taken over by evil. This prayer simply asks God to remove anything that could be in the way of his grace and life, which will be received in baptism.

This prayer also reminds us that the human person is affected by original sin and comes into a world that is already marked by sin. This does not mean that the human person is bad. On the contrary, God has made man and woman 'very good' and delights in everyone one of those he has created and destined to enjoy his love and his glory. Yet the evidence and damage of sin in human life is unavoidable. Only the grace of God can save us from evil. We often find ourselves powerless before its power. Asking for baptism is precisely asking for the salvation from sin, evil and death which we cannot obtain of ourselves, but which only God can give us.

Once the prayer of exorcism has been prayed, the priest anoints the child on the chest with the Oil of the

Catechumens, blessed by the bishop, to strengthen the child. This is a very ancient tradition in the Church: after casting the power of evil, the person is strengthened with the power of Christ. The priest prays as the anointing takes place:

We anoint you with the oil of salvation in the name of Christ our Saviour; may he strengthen you with his power, who lives and reigns for ever and ever. **Amen.**

After this, the child is ready for baptism.

Blessing and invocation of God over the baptismal water

"I tell you most solemnly, unless a man is born through water and the Spirit, he cannot enter the kingdom of God." (*John* 3:5)

The priest, parents and child and the godparents all gather together next to the baptismal font, which is the recipient for the water which will be used for baptism.

The priest will pray a prayer over the waters, which will be consecrated for the baptism. In the course of this prayer, he will invite the people to respond **Amen** or **Blessed be God**. There are different prayers to choose from. All recall the saving actions of God: the love of the Father, the sacrifice of his Son, Jesus Christ, and the sending of the Gift of the Holy Spirit.

The different forms of prayer will all end with a blessing of the water, asking the Father through his Son to send the

Holy Spirit upon the water and make it holy.

> *May the power of the Holy Spirit,*
> *O Lord, we pray,*
> *come down through your Son*
> *into the fullness of this font,*
> *so that all who have been buried with Christ*
> *by Baptism into death*
> *may rise again to life with him.*
> *Who lives and reigns with you*
> > *in the unity of the Holy Spirit,*
> *one God, for ever and ever.*
> **Amen.**

The renunciation of sin

"I will leave this place and go to my Father and say:
Father, I have sinned against heaven and against you" ...
> *So he left the place and went back to his Father.*
> (*Luke* 15:18-20)

After the blessing of the water, the baptismal promises take place. They are divided in two parts: the renunciation of sin and the profession of faith.

The priest will remind parents and godparents how important these promises are with these words:

Dear parents and godparents: You have come here to present this child for baptism. By water and the Holy Spirit he/she is to receive the gift of new life from God, who is love.

On your part, you must make it your constant care to bring him/her up in the practice of the faith. See that the divine life which God gives him/her is kept safe from the poison of sin, to grow always stronger in his/her heart.

If your faith makes you ready to accept this responsibility, renew now the vows of your own baptism. Reject sin; profess your faith in Christ Jesus. This is the faith of the Church. This is the faith in which this child is about to be baptised.

The renunciation of sin now takes place. There are two equivalent formulas which can be used:

Do you reject Satan? Parents and godparents: **I do.**

And all his works? Parents and godparents: **I do.**

And all his empty promises? Parents and godparents: **I do.**

Or:

Do you reject sin, so as to live in the freedom of God's children? Parents and godparents: I do.

Do you reject the glamour of evil, and refuse to be mastered by sin? Parents and godparents: I do.

Do you reject Satan, father of sin and prince of darkness? Parents and godparents: I do.

The profession of faith

"Do you believe in the Son of Man?"
"Sir," the man replied, "tell me who he is so that I may
believe in him." Jesus said, "You are looking at him;
he is speaking to you." The man said, "Lord, I believe",
and worshipped him. (John 9:35-38)

After the renunciation of sin comes the profession of faith. "Baptism is the sacrament of faith."[4] The profession of faith is threefold: we believe in God who is Father, Son and Holy Spirit. This faith is the faith of the Church which has been handed down to us through the ages, starting with the Apostles who are the witnesses of the death and resurrection of Jesus Christ and who transmitted Jesus's own life and teaching to us. The Church keeps the faith and hands on the faith of the Apostles to everyone. Now the parents and godparents who have received this faith and believe it, profess it, and commit themselves to hand on this faith to the child who is to be baptised.

Here is the profession of faith:

Do you believe in God, the Father almighty,
creator of heaven and earth?

Parents and godparents: **I do.**

---

[4] *Catechism of the Catholic Church*, 1253

Do you believe in Jesus Christ,
his only Son, our Lord,
who was born of the Virgin Mary,
was crucified, died, and was buried,
rose from the dead,
and is now seated at the right hand of the Father?
Parents and godparents: **I do.**

Do you believe in the Holy Spirit,
the holy catholic Church,
the communion of saints,
the forgiveness of sins,
the resurrection of the body,
and the life everlasting?
Parents and godparents: **I do.**

This is our faith.
This is the faith of the Church.
We are proud to profess it, in Christ Jesus our Lord.
All: **Amen.**

If there are any articles of the faith which seem obscure, or about which you are not sure, you can always ask your priest about it, and discuss the matter so as to come to a clearer understanding.

The baptism

"Go therefore, make disciples of all the nations;
baptise them in the name of the Father and of the Son
and of the Holy Spirit." (Matthew 28:19)

After the promises - renunciation of sin and profession of faith - have been made, the baptism takes place very simply.

The parents and godparents are asked one last time:

*Is it your will that **N.** should be baptised in the faith of the Church, which we have all professed with you?*

If this is what they truly desire for their child, they answer: **It is.**

Then the child is baptised. This is done either by pouring water over the child three times or by immersion: plunging the child in the water three times. 'To baptise' comes from a Greek word which means 'to plunge' or 'to immerse' in water.

N., *I baptise you in the name of the Father,*

He immerses the child or pours water upon it.

and of the Son,

He immerses the child or pours water upon it a second time.

and of the Holy Spirit.

He immerses the child or pours water upon it a third time.

Through this simple action and word, the salvation of God in Jesus Christ is extended to the child, who becomes at that moment a child of the Father, one with the Son, a temple of the Holy Spirit and a member of the Church. This follows the command of our Lord Jesus Christ who said to his disciples:

"All authority in heaven and on earth has been given to me. Go, therefore, make disciples of all the nations; baptise them in the name of the Father and of the Son and of the Holy Spirit, and teach them to observe all the commands I gave you. And know that I am with you always; yes, to the end of time." (*Matthew* 28:18-20)

The anointing with chrism

"You have been anointed by the Holy One,
and have all received the knowledge." (1 *John* 2:20)

The baptism is followed by the anointing with chrism. Chrism is a sacred oil, which has been consecrated by the bishop and which signifies the gift of the Holy Spirit, who is poured out on the child. This is the prayer of the anointing with Chrism:

The God of power and Father of our Lord Jesus Christ
has freed you from sin,
given you a new birth by water and the Holy Spirit,

and welcomed you into his holy people.
He now anoints you with the chrism of salvation.
As Christ was anointed Priest, Prophet, and King,
so may you live always as a member of his body,
sharing everlasting life.
All: **Amen.**

Then the celebrant anoints the child on the crown of the head with the sacred chrism, in silence.

Jesus is the 'Christ': the 'Anointed' of the Father. 'Christ' means 'Anointed', and Christians are those who share in the anointing of Jesus Christ. They receive the 'unction' of the Holy Spirit, who unites them to Jesus and gives them a share in Jesus's own mission to be Priest, Prophet and King in the world. Each Christian shares in this mission. To be Priest with Jesus, means that we are now able to offer a sacrifice of prayer and praise to the Father. To be Prophet with Jesus means that we are now able to proclaim the Word of God to the world. To be King with Jesus means that we share in his kingdom, and are able in him to defeat the power of sin in our lives and in the world, and not be conquered by it.

Later on, the baptised child will be able to receive freely the sacrament of confirmation. The Holy Spirit will be poured afresh and confirm him or her in the grace of baptism.

The clothing with a white garment

All baptised in Christ, you have all clothed yourselves in Christ. (*Galatians* 3:27)

As a sign of the new life received in Jesus Christ through the Holy Spirit, the child is now clothed in a white garment. The white garment signifies that the newly baptised person has now 'put on Christ'. The child has passed from darkness into light, and lives now as a new creature in union with the risen Christ.

N., *you have become a new creation,*
and have clothed yourself in Christ.
See in this white garment the outward sign of your
Christian dignity.
With your family and friends to help you by word
and example,
bring that dignity unstained
into the everlasting life of heaven.
All: **Amen.**

The white garment is put on the child.

The parents or godparents clothe the child with the white garment, which they have prepared beforehand for this moment. It can be put on over the child's clothes.

The giving of the lighted candle

"I am the light of the world; anyone who follows me will not be walking in the dark; he will have the light of life."
(*John* 8:12)

The parents and godparents now receive a candle on behalf of the child. At this point, the great Easter candle is brought in. It has been lit from the beginning. The Easter candle is the great candle used during the Easter Vigil. It is lit from the Easter fire, blessed by the priest, and it represents the risen Christ, the Light that shines in the darkness of the world.

The priest tells the child: *Receive the light of Christ.*

Someone from the family (such as the father or godfather) lights the child's candle from the Easter candle.

The priest then says:

Parents and godparents,
this light is entrusted to you to be kept burning brightly.
This child of yours has been enlightened by Christ.
He/she is to walk always as a child of the light.
May he/she keep the flame of faith alive in his/her heart.
When the Lord comes, may he/she go out to meet him
with all the saints in the heavenly kingdom.

Jesus Christ is the Light of the world. All the baptised who are united to him through faith and love in the communion of the Church become in their turn the light of the world. The baptismal candle is a sign that your child is now a member of Christ, who brings the light of Jesus into the world.

After the giving of the lighted candle, there may be a last prayer prayed over the child. During this prayer, the priest touches the ears and mouth of the child with his thumb, saying:

The Lord Jesus made the deaf hear and the dumb speak.
May he soon touch your ears to receive his word,
and your mouth to proclaim his faith,
to the praise and glory of God the Father.
All: **Amen.**

As a baptised member of Jesus Christ and of the Church, the child can now grow into the fullness of life in the Church, with access to all the other sacraments.

How is Baptism Lived Day-to-Day?

At baptism, we receive three supernatural gifts, three 'superpowers' called 'theological virtues': faith, hope and charity. These gifts from God enable us to live our baptism call day to day, in the knowledge, trust and love of God. The invisible realities that faith enables us to know, hope enables us to trust and charity enables us to love. At baptism, we receive the supernatural abilities to know God, to trust God and to love God.

A Life of Faith

I live now not with my own life but with the life of Christ who lives in me. The life I now live in this body I live in faith: faith in the Son of God who loved me and who sacrificed himself for my sake. (Galatians 2:20)

Baptism is the beginning of a life of faith in God.

To have faith means to believe everything that the Father has revealed to us in Jesus Christ, which has been faithfully handed on to us through the Church filled with the Holy Spirit. This 'content' of the faith - what we believe - is summarised in the Creed, the profession of faith[5] which parents make at baptism and which we make every Sunday.

[5] See the profession of faith on p. 52.

Thanks to the active presence of the Holy Spirit who has been given to the Church at Pentecost and has never left since, the truth of the faith is kept faithfully, and is passed on to all generations of believers. The teachings of the popes, bishops and priests help us to understand more fully God's revelation and to live according to it more faithfully.

To have faith also means that we know God as a friend, that we have put our complete trust in God's personal love for us. It means that we have a relationship with God who is Father, Son and Holy Spirit. We do not believe in God simply as a matter of acknowledging the truth about a God we cannot see, just as we acknowledge that William the Conqueror invaded England in 1066, or that light is made out of photons, even though we cannot see these things for ourselves. Our faith in God involves our whole being, our whole existence. Through faith, we know God in the same way as we know the reality of the love of our family and friends, and even with more certainty than that. Through faith, we know that God's love for us will never fail and will never run short. Human love is always limited. God's love is infinite and absolute. Through faith, God becomes an essential presence in our life, and faith in him becomes part of ourselves. This changes the whole perspective of our life. We constantly grow in our relationship with God, in our faith in him.

At baptism, we receive the gift of faith, which enables us to know God. This knowledge of God is supernatural: a gift of God which we didn't have at birth, but which we are given at baptism to enable us to enter into this relationship with Father, Son and Holy Spirit.

Like any gift, natural or supernatural, the gift of faith given at baptism grows as we use it. It grows every time we make an act of faith. An act of faith is an action which involves our personal 'yes' to God and our personal, certain knowledge of God. Praying, reading Scripture, going to church, receiving the sacraments, loving others in obedience to God's commandments are all acts of faith, which will enable our faith to grow and flourish.

Like any gift, the gift of faith will wither and possibly die if we never use it. Parents should be attentive to provide opportunities for their children's faith to grow by teaching the faith, praying together as a family, and participating in the life of their faith community: the parish.

Baptism is the beginning of our life of faith. This life of faith is nourished throughout our lives especially in the sacraments of the Church. Every time we receive the sacraments with a right attitude, the gift of faith grows in us: our faith becomes stronger. This is why attending Mass weekly is so important for our faith.

As you remain faithful in the Church, your child will grow in faith. When the time for receiving the sacrament of confirmation comes, your child will be able to understand and co-operate more fully with the grace of God, active in him or her since baptism. In the sacrament of confirmation, given some years after infant baptism in the Roman Catholic Church, we are strengthened in faith, hope and charity and we receive the seven gifts of the Holy Spirit. In this sacrament, the Holy Spirit will confirm your child in the faith received at baptism. This will also be an opportunity for your child to make a personal response of faith to the gift of God received at baptism. Parents preparing for the baptism of their child should have the intention of helping their child to discover and desire the other sacraments of the Church, which will be available throughout their lives, and which will help them to grow in faith.

A Life of Hope

Hope is not deceptive, because the love of God has been poured into our hearts by the Holy Spirit which has been given us. (*Romans* 5:5)

At baptism, your child will receive the gift of hope. How can hope be a gift? The hope we receive at baptism is not an ordinary kind of hope. Ordinary hope gives us a positive outlook on life, and a positive expectation of the good things to come in this life, i.e.: "I hope that the weather will be good"; "I hope to succeed in my exams"; "I hope to recover from this illness"; "I hope to meet someone who will love me..." The kind of hope we receive at baptism is different: it is hope in God. It is the supernatural ability to trust God no matter what, even in the darkest situations of life.

Whereas the supernatural gift of faith enables us to know with certainty God whom we cannot see, the supernatural gift of hope enables us to trust completely in God's plan of love for us. The realities that hope enables us to trust are God, God's love and care for the Church and for each one of us personally (which we call 'providence'), and the reality of eternal life with God, a life that endures beyond the physical separation of death.

Thanks to supernatural hope, we are able to face suffering, difficulties, sin, earthly disappointments, bereavement, and even physical death. This does not mean that difficulties or suffering disappear. It means that we become able to face them without despairing, looking to God and to his love, which has become the foundation of our life at baptism.

Like faith and charity, the gift of hope can wither and even die in us if we do use it, if we do not put it in practice. How do we use our hope? How do we put hope in practice? Every action relating to the practice of our Faith is 'fuelled' by hope. Faith gives a direction to our actions, and hope gives them a motivation. Without hope, we wouldn't do anything: we may believe in God, but there would be no reason to go to Church, no reason to help others, no reason to pray, no reason to forgive anyone or to ask for God's forgiveness. We would expect nothing, and look forward to nothing. Without hope, we wouldn't consider as real the possibility of an eternal future, and the possibility of change for the better in this life, either in ourselves or in others, and so we would have no reason to act with love. It is when we stop acting in the perspective of God's love for us and for all people, and in the perspective of our eternal future with him - preferring the here and now to his call, for example on Sunday morning when it is time to go and worship him in Church - that we begin to lose our supernatural hope.

Hope fills every one of the decisions and actions which direct us towards God. In fact, hope is the reason you are asking for your child to receive baptism: you are hoping in God by entrusting your child to him, and hoping in God's gift of eternal life for your child.

Hope founded on God assures us that we have a future beyond physical death. Hope also tells us that the possibility for anyone to change for the best through God's grace - ourselves included - is ever present. Hope does not know any 'closed' situation, any human situation of total darkness, because it trusts in the all-powerful, all-loving grace of God, which was displayed on the cross, the darkest of situations. Hope lives and acts in the light of the resurrection of Jesus Christ.

Hope in particular enables us to believe that God can make a change and difference in our lives, in the knowledge that every saint (except Mary, the Mother of Jesus) started life as a sinner. This confidence and trust in God's grace and mercy, which is hope, is the reason why we go to confession.

Confession is the sacrament that reconciles us to God. We come to God with our burden of sins and lay it down at the foot of the cross in complete honesty. Then we receive the forgiveness of God: a new baptism, a clean slate to start afresh. Each time we receive the sacrament of reconciliation, we are renewed and strengthened in faith, hope and charity. Asking for and receiving God's forgiveness and grace in the sacrament of reconciliation is one of the greatest acts of supernatural hope and human courage we can make.

Prayer, which is the raising of our hearts and minds to God, is also impossible to do without hope.

Through prayer, we enter directly in touch with God. We enter into a conversation and intimacy of love with him. We contemplate the face of Jesus Christ - the human face of God. If we had no hope, we would have no reason to pray, and no reason to ask God for our needs and the needs of the world.

A Life of Charity

"If anyone loves me he will keep my word,
and my Father will love him, and we shall come to him
and make our home with him." (John 14:23)

"God is love" (*1 John* 4:8). God is Father, Son and Holy Spirit, an eternal communion of love. At baptism, "the love of God has been poured into our hearts by the Holy Spirit who has been given to us" (*Romans* 5:5). We call the love of God we receive in baptism 'charity'. Charity is the supernatural ability to respond with love to God's love for us, and to love others as Jesus has loved us. Supernatural charity makes us sharers in God's own life and being, since God is love.

How is charity put into practice? We know and enjoy a natural kind of love in this life: love for our family and friends, love for those who love us. Charity enables us to love at a deeper, wider level. It enables us to love God whom we cannot see, and to love others in a deeper way, not because we necessarily enjoy their company, or because they can return our love, but simply by considering them as brothers and sisters in Jesus Christ, infinitely loved and willed by God who creates each one of us uniquely.

It is charity which enables us to bear patiently those who tend to annoy or even hurt us, to act kindly towards all equally, to forgive wrongs readily and from the heart, to act courageously in defence of those who are oppressed, to help those in need, to offer our time and ears to those who are in need of care and friendship...

St Paul famously tells us what charity enables us to do:

Love is always patient and kind; it is never jealous; love is never boastful or conceited; it is never rude or selfish; it does not take offence, and is not resentful. Love takes no pleasure in other people's sins but delights in the truth; it is always ready to excuse, to trust, to hope and to endure whatever comes. (*1 Corinthians* 13:4-7)

The supernatural gift of charity transforms us into the image of Jesus Christ, and enables us to see Jesus Christ in our brothers and sisters.

Through Charity, every one of our actions, even the most ordinary, becomes an act of love and is lifted up to the level of God who is love. By acting with charity, we freely contribute to the great outpouring of God's love which has been released in the world since the coming of God the Son as man in Jesus Christ. Our capacity to love others in the way that Jesus loved us: by forgiving and giving our lives for others, is a witness to God's love and presence. We would not be able to do this without God's grace and presence in our life.

The Church is the communion of men and women who have accepted the love of God in their lives and been transformed by it. We receive this love at Church every Sunday in the Eucharist, the Body and Blood of Jesus Christ, which is the sacrament of charity, the sacrament of love.

At Mass, the unique sacrifice of the cross is made present for us. The cross is God's gift of himself for us: on the cross, God the Son, Jesus Christ, offered his life as a sacrifice for sins, to reconcile us to the Father. Thanks to the cross and resurrection of Jesus and the outpouring of the Holy Spirit into our hearts, we are able to enter into the communion of love of Father, Son and Holy Spirit. At Mass, Jesus offers his life for us: "This is my body, which will be given for you...This is my blood, which will be poured out for you" (Luke 22:19-20). We receive his life into our own lives through Holy Communion. Holy Communion is our own communion with Father, Son and Holy Spirit, a union of love. Holy Communion also means that we are in communion - in union - with each other. The bond of this communion is charity.

We can refuse to enter or to remain in this communion of charity, which is the Church, by knowingly and willingly committing a grave sin against God or against another. We can simply stop remaining in this communion by not going to Mass on Sunday. When we know that we have broken the bond of communion with God and with the Church by our action, it can always be restored through God's mercy in the sacrament of reconciliation.

A Life in the Family of the Church

The whole group of believers was united, heart and soul.
(Acts 4:32)

A life of faith, hope and charity can never be lived alone: we cannot believe in God, trust in God and love God and each other on our own. To be faithful to the promises you are about to make on behalf of your child, the support and help of the parish community will be indispensable.

The parish is your local Catholic community, where all the baptised Catholics who live locally are called to attend Mass and form bonds of fellowship together, led by the priest in charge of the parish. As a preparation for your child's baptism and to help you provide an environment where your child's faith, hope and love will grow, make sure you get to know well your parish, your priest and some of the parishioners who attend Mass on Sunday, and who often meet the same challenges as you will in maintaining a life of faithfulness to the Catholic faith.

The sacraments of the Church - God's life and grace made available to us through baptism, confirmation, the Eucharist (Mass), confession, the sacrament of the sick, marriage - are all available in your parish, through the ministry of the priest who has received the sacrament of Holy Orders, which give him the power and authority to act in the Person of Christ.

The parish will no doubt offer opportunities for you to nurture your own faith, so that you will be able to help your child grow in his or her own faith. This is done through parish study groups, Bible-sharing groups, events and courses, talks and conferences.

The parish will offer opportunities to exercise hope in prayer: not only in the celebration of Mass, but also in other ways: in lighting candles, in a rosary group, adoration of the Blessed Sacrament, and in prayer groups which can often meet in parishes. Praying together can often help us develop the taste for prayer and a habit of prayer.

The parish will also offer opportunities to grow in charity: through service of others in various groups or initiatives (SVP, CAFOD, Aid to the Church in Need, local charities' initiatives...) but also through fellowship and friendship with other members of the parish in social events and in reaching out to other parish members who may be in need of help and friendship.

It is only as you live your own baptism in your local community of baptised members of Jesus Christ - the parish - that you will be able to help your child grow in faithfulness to his or her own baptism.

How Can We Prepare For It?

Baptism is God's gift to us, and it is a gift you desire your child to receive. It will be one of the most significant events in the life of your child, who will become adopted by the Father and receive the salvation from sin and death offered by Jesus Christ through the Holy Spirit. This irreversible gift will mark your child for ever as a child of God and a member of the Catholic Church.

Preparing for it is essential. Here are a few suggestions. Some may be helpful, and some may seem burdensome. Choose the ones that will help you best in your particular circumstances. Choose the one that you will be able to manage without too much difficulty.

Prayers

Together and/or on your own, prepare for the baptism of your child by praying regularly for God's grace on your family and particularly for your child who is about to receive God in his or her life.

- First, you can pray a simple prayer of protection and blessing for your child, in your own words or using the words below. You can do this every day until the baptism.

Heavenly Father, we ask you to bless and protect our family.

Fill us with your wisdom to make the best decision for our beloved child.

We ask for the help and presence of your Holy Spirit in our hearts as we prepare for the baptism. Help us to understand what you give us and to be faithful to your gift of love.

We make this prayer through Jesus Christ your beloved Son our Lord. **Amen.**

Here are simple, essential Catholic prayers, which you can pray regularly as a family or on your own, to foster in the family the grace of baptism:

- The 'Our Father' is the prayer of all the baptised, all those who are adopted children of the Father. Jesus himself taught us to call God 'Father'.

  Our Father, Who art in heaven
  Hallowed be Thy Name;
  Thy kingdom come,
  Thy will be done,
  on earth as it is in heaven.
  Give us this day our daily bread,
  and forgive us our trespasses,
  as we forgive those who trespass against us;

and lead us not into temptation,
but deliver us from evil.
Amen.

• The 'Hail Mary' is addressed to our Mother Mary, asking her to pray for her children. As we become one with Jesus in baptism, Mary becomes our Mother.

Hail Mary, full of grace. The Lord is with thee.
Blessed art thou amongst women,
and blessed is the fruit of thy womb, Jesus.
Holy Mary, Mother of God,
pray for us sinners,
now and at the hour of our death.
Amen.

• The 'Glory be' is a short prayer of praise and adoration to God the Blessed Trinity who is Father, Son and Holy Spirit. As baptised members of Christ, we are called to give glory to God the Trinity now in this life and forever in heaven.

Glory be to the Father,
and to the Son,
and to the Holy Spirit,
as it was in the beginning,
is now, and ever shall be,
world without end.
Amen.

- The profession of our faith can also be spoken as a prayer. It reminds us of God, who he is and what he has done for us. The profession of faith - the Apostles' Creed below - has been proclaimed and prayed by baptised Christians since the beginning of the Church.

I believe in God,
the Father almighty,
Creator of heaven and earth,
and in Jesus Christ, his only Son, our Lord,
who was conceived by the Holy Spirit,
born of the Virgin Mary,
suffered under Pontius Pilate,
was crucified, died and was buried;
he descended into hell;
on the third day he rose again from the dead;
he ascended into heaven,
and is seated at the right hand of God
    the Father almighty;
from there he will come to judge the living
    and the dead.
I believe in the Holy Spirit,
the holy catholic Church,
the communion of saints,
the forgiveness of sins,
the resurrection of the body,
and life everlasting.
Amen.

- The Prayer of the 'Hail, Holy Queen' is an ancient prayer of the Church to ask for our Mother Mary's help in every difficulty of life.

Hail Holy Queen
Hail, Holy Queen, Mother of mercy,
our life, our sweetness and our hope.
To thee do we cry, poor banished children of Eve:
to thee do we send up our sighs,
mourning and weeping in this valley of tears.
Turn then, most gracious Advocate,
thine eyes of mercy toward us,
and after this our exile,
show unto us the blessed fruit of thy womb, Jesus.
O clement, O loving, O sweet Virgin Mary!
Amen.

Using all the prayers above, you can pray a decade or a full rosary. To help you pray the Rosary, to begin a life of greater faithfulness to prayer, you can find online help by looking at these links:

www.comepraytherosary.org

totus2us.com/prayer

www.pray-as-you-go.org/home/

To pray, simply choose one or more prayers from the list above, and, alone or together, take a time of silence, turning towards God in the depth of your heart. Then pray the prayer(s) you have chosen slowly, thinking about the words you are saying, for yourself and for your child. This can take less than five minutes. Do this every day until the baptism of your child is celebrated. You can build up this habit of prayer in your home afterward, entrusting yourself and your family to God and to the loving intercession of our Mother Mary.

Scripture readings

If you have access to a Bible, either at home, online or through the parish, it is a good idea to begin reading the Word of God to nourish your own faith and love for God. You may be unfamiliar with the Bible. In the list of links below you will find help to access the Bible easily and to find your way around it.

www.ewtn.com/devotionals/biblesearch.asp

www.vatican.va/archive/ENG0839/_INDEX.HTM

Finding your way around the Bible:

www.youtube.com/watch?v=VS51L7jOF6o

Here is a list of suggested readings to help you prepare for the baptism of your child.

Before starting your reading of Scripture, take a moment of silence and ask the Holy Spirit to open your heart and mind, to be able to understand and live the Word of God.

Short Bible readings

Psalm 4; Psalm 8; Psalm 16; Psalm 23; Psalm 34; Psalm 42; Psalm 51; Psalm 103; Psalm 131

The Gospel of St Luke, chapter 3, verses 21-22

St Paul's first letter to the Corinthians, chapter 12, verses 12-13

St Paul's letter to the Colossians, chapter 2, verses 6-15

St Paul's letter to the Colossians, chapter 3, verses 1-17

St Paul's letter to Titus, chapter 3, verses 1-8

Medium Bible readings

The Gospel of St John, chapter 1

The Gospel of St Luke, chapter 5, verses 1-32

The Gospel of St John, chapter 3

The Gospel of St John, chapter 4

The Gospel of St John, chapter 9

The Gospel of St John, chapter 11

St Paul's letter to the Romans, chapter 5

St Paul's letter to the Romans, chapter 6

St Paul's letter to the Romans, chapter 7

St Paul's letter to the Romans, chapter 8

Long Bible readings

The Gospel of St Mark

The Gospel of to St Luke

St Paul's letter to the Philippians

St Paul's letter to the Colossians

St Paul's letter to the Ephesians

The first letter of St Peter

Family activities to prepare for the baptism

Apart from praying and reading the Scripture, there are a few things you can do together that will help you prepare for the baptism and give meaning to what your child is about to receive. Below is a list of non-exhaustive suggestions.

- Preparing/making a white baptismal garment. This needs to be ready for the ceremony. It is easy to find a last minute white baby garment, but it would be so much more meaningful to take time to provide your child with his or her own baptismal robe. Sometimes a baptismal garment is passed on in the family and can be stored away, waiting to be used again.

- A pre-baptism dinner, where you could invite the godparents and think about the meaning of baptism together. You could invite the godparents to read this booklet beforehand and discuss during the dinner aspects which may have struck you or that you want to understand more deeply. You can also invite the parish priest or one of the parish members to answer questions, or search for answers in the YouCat or Catechism (see below).

- Preparing and decorating a unique candle which will serve as your child's baptismal candle. This candle should be long and thin, and can be decorated with symbols of baptism, or with a simple cross.

- Preparing for a cake to be made for a small party after the baptism. This cake could be decorated with the symbols of baptism which have been the most significant for you as you have prepared for the sacrament.

- Making or acquiring a beautiful reminder of the baptism to be placed in the room of your child: a crucifix hanging on the wall, a beautiful certificate in calligraphy signed by the priest, which you would have prepared beforehand, or a meaningful image relating to baptism that you can explain to your child later on. You can ask the priest to bless this particular item.

- Making or ordering a small decorated prayer card which can be given out after the baptism to all the guests, asking them to pray for your child.

- A mini-retreat before the baptism. This can take the form of a visit to the church as a family, to a shrine nearby, or to a place of prayer. It can also be done as an outing into the countryside. During this visit as a family, take time to pray together in silence for a few minutes, and together to ask God to bless your family and to prepare all your hearts to receive his gifts. You can invite the godparents and friends to participate in this outing.

Deepening the family's Catholic faith

A great variety of resources are available for you to deepen your faith, whatever stage you may be.

You will find the essentials of the faith here:

YouCat: www.youcat.org

Compendium of the Catechism of the Catholic Church:

www.vatican.va/archive/compendium_ccc/documents/ archive_2005_compendium-ccc_en.html

Catechism of the Catholic Church:

www.scborromeo.org/ccc.htm

All of these are available for purchase from the Catholic Truth Society: *www.ctsbooks.org*

Through the Catholic Truth Society, you will find a whole range of booklets and courses on different areas of the faith that will help you deepen your understanding and love for God.

One such course, which can be done in the parish or in the home, is Anchor: Anchoring you in New Life, a course which explains and deepens the meaning of baptism: *www.anchoryourfaith.com*

Faith in the Family

Anne Burke-Gaffney & Fr Marcus Holden

Divided into three themes: 'Creation and created', 'Knowing God' and 'Catholic life and times', questions and answers are expressed in language that can be easily communicated by parents to children and then translated into action and supported with prayers, activities and practical suggestions.

This book will help parents to live and pass on the Catholic Faith within their families in a lively and practical way, and give them the confidence to answer the numerous and often challenging faith-related questions that children ask.

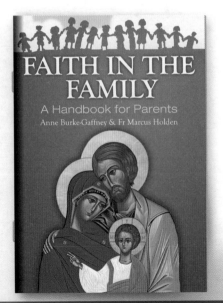

PA 18   ISBN 978 1 86082 860 7

Baptism - New Life in Christ

Sr Eustochium

Baptism involves the use of ordinary things-water, oil, white garments, lighted candles-which carry a specific significance, some of which seem obvious while others take a bit of unpacking. The purpose of this booklet is to provide an introduction to baptism in the Catholic Church, looking both at the practicalities of baptism and at its history and meaning.

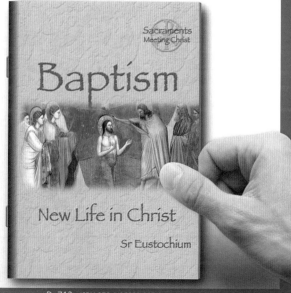

Do712   ISBN 978 1 86082 232 2

Passing on Faith to Your Children

Peter Kahn

At baptism a very great task is entrusted to parents by the Church: namely to pass on the living faith to their children. What does this involve, and how can parents work together to meet their responsibilities. This booklet explores what kind of faith we are to pass on to our children, and then gives practical help on how to best give children a positive, rich and complete experinece of Catholic Christianity

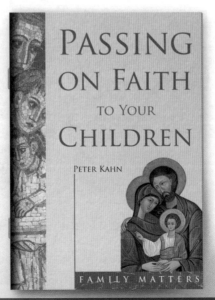

PA6   ISBN 978 1 86082 391 6

Effective Parenting

James B. Stenson

This text sets out the importance of the role parents have and shows how that role must be expressed through nurturing and encouraging one's children along a path to responsible caring adulthood.

Giving pointers on such subjects as: the interaction between parents, the setting of rules, the building of a family unit, how to communicate with both small and adolescent children, what the ultimate goal of effective parenting should be, and much more, it willbe a great help for even the most experienced mothers and fathers and novices alike.

PA19   ISBN 978 1 86082 866 9